GW01336698

Hardback edition first published in Great Britain 1983 by
Hamish Hamilton Children's Books
Garden House, 57–59 Long Acre, London WC2E 9JZ

Paperback edition first published 1985

British Library Cataloguing in Publication Data
Snell, Nigel
Jenny learns to swim
I. Title
823'.914[J] PZ7
ISBN 0-241-11026-2 (hardback)
ISBN 0-241-11461-6 (paperback)

Printed in Great Britain by
Cambus Litho, East Kilbride

Jenny learns to Swim

NIGEL SNELL

Hamish Hamilton · London

Jenny and her mummy were eating breakfast.
'Do you remember what we are doing today?'
asked mummy.
Jenny shook her head.
'We are going to the swimming pool
for your first swimming lesson.'

Jenny was very excited,
but also a little scared.
She wasn't sure she liked water.

That afternoon, they went to the pool and met Mr Trout.
He was the swimming teacher.

Jenny changed into her swimming things.
She said hello to the other girls
and boys.
Mr Trout told them to get into the water.

It only came up to Jenny's waist.

Mr Trout asked everyone to hold onto the bar at the side of the pool.
He told them to kick
with their legs out behind them.

‘Very good Jenny,’ he said.

Next, he gave them each a float.
The children put them under their arms
and kicked with their legs.

First, all the girls had to
swim across the pool.
Then all the boys.

Mr Trout showed them
how to do ‘dog paddle’.
‘Keep your fingers tight together’,
he said.
He made them practise
by walking across the pool.

Jenny wasn’t at all scared.
And the water was lovely and warm!

Then Mr Trout got into the water
to help the children swim.
He put his hand under their tummies
to stop them from sinking.

Jenny was scared at first.
She though she might swallow
a lot of water.
But Mr Trout made sure
she swam safely across.

Then they all swam back,
this time on their backs.
'Give yourselves a clap,' he said.
'You have all been very clever.'

CLAP
CLAP
CLAP
CLAP
CLAP
CLAP

Just before they went home,
Mr Trout let them play some games.
He gave them some rings and ping pong
balls to throw to each other in the water.
It was great fun!

Then Mr Trout made them
jump up and down
and put their heads
right under the water.

Jenny went to swimming classes twice a week.
She learned to do breast-stroke like a little frog.

And one day, when mummy came to collect her, Jenny swam the whole length of the pool.

Mummy was very proud!

The End